791.6

Penworthy

1000

2-2016

☆ CHEER SPIRIT ☆

JUMP, TUCK, FLIP

Mastering Cheerleading Skills and Stunts

by Rebecca Rissman

Consultant:
Tara L. Wieland
Owner and Head Coach
Michigan Storm Cheer and Dance
Midland, Michigan

CAPSTONE PRESS
a capstone imprint

Snap Books are published by Capstone Press,
1710 Roe Crest Drive, North Mankato, Minnesota 56003
www.capstonepub.com

Library of Congress Cataloging-in-Publication Data
    Rissman, Rebecca.
 Jump, tuck, flip : mastering cheerleading skills and stunts / by Rebecca
Rissman.
     pages cm. — (Cheer Spirit)
 Includes webography.
 Includes bibliographical references and index.
  Audience: Age: 8–14.
 ISBN 978-1-4914-5203-5 (library binding)
 ISBN 978-1-4914-5219-6 (eBook PDF)
 1. Cheers—Juvenile literature. 2. Cheerleading—Juvenile literature. I. Title.
  LB3635.R55 2016
  791.6'4—d23
                              2015009413

Editorial Credits
Abby Colich, editor; Heidi Thompson, designer; Tracy Cummins,
media researcher; Katy LaVigne, production specialist

Photo Credits
Capstone Press: Karon Dubke, 6, 7, 8, 9, 10, 11, 12, 13, 14, 15, 21, 23, 24, 25, 26,
27, 28, 29, 30; Corbis: Tony Anderson, 17; Getty Images: Tony Anderson, 19;
Newscom: Doug Murray/Icon SMI, 5; Shutterstock: Robert Adrian Hillman,
Design Element, surachet khamsuk, Design Element, zsooofija, Design
Element; SuperStock: Exactostock-1527, 16; Thinkstock: Mike Powell, Cover

Printed in the United States of America in North Mankato, Minnesota.
052015   008823CGF15

TABLE OF CONTENTS

READY? OK!

Picture this. It's the fourth quarter of the big game. The score is tied, and the team needs a boost. You know just what to do. Your cheerleading squad begins to perform amazing flips. Then you start to chant "GO BIG BLUE!" Soon the crowd is chanting along. It's so loud you can hardly hear. Suddenly your team scores! It's a win!

Cheerleaders use many different stunts and skills to excite the crowd. Stunts and skills also wow judges during competitions. Cheerleading movements are choreographed to match different cheers, chants, and songs. Some are simple, such as marching in place. Others are amazing feats of acrobatics. Advanced cheerleading squads combine gymnastics, acrobatics, and daring jumps with their chants and cheers.

There are awesome stunts and skills for cheerleaders of all levels. Even the simplest moves wow the crowd when performed with good form and in unison.

Be safe! Never do a cheerleading motion, stunt, tumble, or jump that causes you pain. Make sure to practice any stunts, tumbling, or jumps with a coach or adult first. A coach will make sure you do each move safely and correctly.

GET IN LINE!

Before cheerleaders can flip upside down, they have to learn where to stand right side up. Different formations help cheerleaders use their space wisely. On a football field, they might form a long line so that they can cheer to fans all along the stands. On a basketball court, they might form a diamond during their halftime routine. There are many different formations a squad may use.

BOWLING PIN

The Bowling Pin allows for cheerleaders to be on different levels. Cheerleaders in the front rows may be on their knees or bending down.

Before you do any cheerleading moves, always warm up and stretch. This will help prevent injuries. First do 5 to 10 minutes of cardio activity. Doing jumping jacks or running in place will get blood flowing to your muscles. Then make sure to stretch, but not too much. If you overstretch, your muscles won't be able to keep you stable when tumbling and jumping. Do simple stretches for about 10 minutes. You can do more flexibility exercises and stretching after your workout.

WINDOWS

In the Windows formation, the crowd can see each cheerleader. The rows are staggered so that each cheerleader has enough space to move safely without touching one another.

DIAGONALS

Diagonals help show off a squad's sharp movements. Lining up in diagonal lines lets each part of the crowd see something different. Some fans will see single-file lines. Others will see evenly spaced cheerleaders.

B-A-S-I-C LEARN THESE BASICS 1-2-3!

Every cheerleading routine starts with some simple, basic motions. Learn these positions first. Once these are mastered, you'll be ready for more advanced cheerleading.

READY POSITION

Most cheers and chants begin with the Ready Position. To do this, stand with your feet together and your hands straight down at your sides in blades or fists.

Hand Positions

When you're not holding pom-poms, your hand position is very important. There are three basic hand positions in cheerleading. In all of these, keep your wrists straight.

Fist Ball your hand up tightly with your thumb on the outside.

Blade Make your palm flat and straight with your fingers pressed together.

Jazz Hands (also known as Spirit Fingers) Spread your fingers wide and very quickly shake them.

HIGH V

High V is a very common motion. All you do is stand with your feet a little more than shoulder width apart. Extend your arms up to form a "V" shape. Make fists with your hands, with your pinkies to the back.

With all cheer motions, keep your head looking forward. You should be able to see the motions of your fellow cheerleaders out of the corners of your eyes.

LOW V

Low V is just like High V with one difference. To do Low V, extend your arms down and out to form an upside down "V." Make fists with your hands, with your pinkies to the back.

L POSITION

The L Position is another common motion. Simply bring one arm straight up with the hand in a fist, with the pinkie facing forward. Bring the other arm straight out to the side with the hand in a fist, with the pinkie facing back.

TOUCHDOWN

In football a touchdown earns the team six points. To do the Touchdown motion, stand with your feet about 2 feet (61 centimeters) apart. Bring both arms straight up with the hands in fists.

CHEER TIP!

Make your pom-poms pop! When holding a position, shake and ruffle your pom-poms. They will catch the light and the attention of the crowd.

PUNCH

The Punch means power. In this position stand with your feet about 2 feet (61 cm) apart. Put one hand on your hip. Raise the opposite hand into Touchdown.

Mirror, Mirror

In cheerleading, seeing is believing. Some squads often practice in front of a large mirror. The squad works together to make sure everyone is hitting the same angles and leg positions in each motion. Standing in a single-file line helps everyone see one another's movements.

DIAGONAL

The Diagonal looks just like it sounds. In this motion stand with your feet about 2 feet (61 cm) apart. Extend one arm up into High V. Bring the other down into Low V. Your thumbs should face the front on both arms.

Make sure to keep your wrists straight. Also remember to keep your elbows and knees either very straight or bent at the correct angle for the motion. Slightly bent elbows, knees, or wrists will look sloppy.

T POSITION

The T Position is another common motion. Start by standing with your feet about 2 feet (61 cm) apart. Extend both arms to the sides. Your hands should be in fists, with pinkies facing back.

HALF T POSITION

For Half T Position, start by standing in T Position. Then bend your elbows to bring your fists to your shoulders. Your thumbs should face inward.

DAGGERS

Daggers are a continuation of T and Half T. From Half T Position, bring your elbows down to your sides.

JUMP IT UP!

Jumps are a great way to add some gymnastics into a cheer routine. Jumps can be simple and easy, or advanced and tricky. A coach or adult can help you learn them.

PREP POSITION

(also called a T Jump)

Most jumps need a "prep" or a way for you to get high up into the air first. Here is one common prep. Master this prep before you attempt any other jumps.

1. Start in Ready Position.

2. Bend your knees deeply as if you are going to sit in a chair. Keep your chest upright. Clasp your hands under your chin in front of your chest.

3. Straighten your legs and come onto the balls of your feet. Punch your arms straight up into Touchdown motion. Make your body as tall as possible. Stay in a straight line with your arms slightly in front of you.

4. Bend your knees deeply once more. Swing your arms down in front of your face, toward your knees. Then separate your hands and swing your arms up and out into T Position.

TUCK JUMP

This basic jump is great for beginners.

1. Begin with the Prep.

2. Spring up into the air. Pull both knees into your chest. At the same time, swing your arms into High V.

3. Land with your legs together, knees bent, and your arms down at your sides.

Keep your back safe during jumps. To do this, pull your belly button in toward your spine. Keep your back as straight as you can.

Start slowly! Very few people can do these jumps right away. In fact, they often take months and even years of work. Practice often until you have the flexibility needed to perform each jump. A coach or adult can help you in your practice. And always make sure you practice jumps in wide, open areas.

TOE TOUCH

The Toe Touch requires a lot of flexibility. If you can't get your legs straight at first, keep practicing.

1. Begin with the Prep.

2. Spring up into the air. Pull both legs up from the floor using your hip muscles. Your legs should be straight out to your sides. Your toes should be pointed, chest up tall, and knees facing upward or behind you. At the same time, snap your arms out into T Position. Keep your chest and shoulders lifted upright.

3. Snap your legs underneath you, with your ankles and knees together, knees bent, and hands down at your sides. You should land on the balls of your feet.

Stretch!

Stretch daily to work toward the best form in a toe touch. Each morning warm up with jumping jacks or another cardio activity. Then sit on a flat surface with both legs outstretched. Separate your legs as wide as you can. Keep your toes pointed upward. Then very slowly walk your fingers forward on the ground between your legs. When you feel the stretch intensely, stop and hold for five breaths.

RIGHT HURDLER

The Right Hurdler is similar to the Toe Touch, but only uses one leg. You can also try the Left Hurdler, lifting your left leg into the air.

1. Begin with the Prep.

2. Spring up into the air. Kick your right leg up into a Toe Touch. Bend your left knee out to the left side with your left foot close to your bottom. At the same time, swing your arms forward into Touchdown. Your front foot should be in between your arms.

3. To land, snap your legs underneath you with your ankles and knees together, knees bent, and hands down at your sides. You should land on the balls of your feet.

BUILD A STUNT TEAM

Some advanced cheerleading squads use amazing stunts to wow the crowds. They spin, flip, and fly through the air. But not all stunts require such acrobatics. Basic stunts are a great way to spice up any cheer routine. Ask a coach or adult to help you or your squad learn these stunts.

Each cheerleader on a stunt team will have one of three different jobs. A coach usually decides who does which job.

Flyers are the cheerleaders who stand or cheer from a lifted position.
Bases are the cheerleaders who support the flyers with their legs, arms, or backs.
Spotters (also called backspotters) stand nearby during stunts and help flyers exit the stunt. Spotters are the most important team members. They are the only ones who can see every spot during any stunt.

When putting stunt teams together, coaches make sure these things are true:

★ Bases are strong enough to support the flyer.

★ The flyer can step up and lock out her legs while pulling her body weight into a hollow position (making the stomach long, it should feel "hollow").

★ The spotter is tall enough to reach the flyer on the bases and strong enough to help support the weight.

Importance of Spotters

Spotters are important cheerleaders during stunts. They stand by in case a stunt goes wrong. The main responsibility of a spotter is to be sure that a flyer's head never hits the ground.

THIGH STAND

The Thigh Stand is one of the most basic cheerleading stunts.

Squad members: one flyer, two bases, and one spotter

1. The two bases stand in lunges with their chests upright. One base's lunging foot should be in front of the other base's lunging foot. The toes of one base should line up with the other base's heel.

2. The flyer places her hands on the inside shoulders of the bases.

3. The flyer steps her right leg up as high as possible onto the "pocket" (the top of thigh) of the base to her right.

4. The flyer locks out her left leg as fast as possible, then steps it high onto the other base's "pocket."

5. The flyer stands up tall into a tight hollow body position, moving her arms into a High V.

6. Each base supports the flyer's feet with her front hand on the toe, pulling the foot toward herself. Then each base places her back hand around the knee of the flyer.

7. The spotter will hold the flyer's waist from behind as she gets into position. While the flyer is in position, the spotter helps pull the weight of the flyer up off the bases.

8. To exit, the bases take their front hands and reach up to the flyer. The flyer will grab the bases' hands with hers. The spotter helps her step down to the ground.

SHOULDER SIT

The Shoulder Sit is another basic stunt. Learning Shoulder Sit will help you get ready for more advanced routines.

Squad members: one base, one flyer, and one spotter

1. The base brings one leg forward into a deep lunge.

2. The flyer stands slightly behind the base. She steps her foot up onto the base's "pocket" (the top of the thigh).

3. The base holds onto the flyer's foot. She wraps her other arm around the flyer's knee to keep it supported.

4. The spotter holds the flyer's waist and supports her as she steps up onto the base's thigh and locks out her leg. The flyer then swings her other leg up and around the base's shoulder.

5. The base stands up and brings her hands to just above the flyer's knees. The base pulls down on the flyer's legs to give her extra support.

6. The flyer wraps her toes behind the base's back and moves her arms into High V.

7. The spotter continues to hold the flyer's waist, pulling up the weight of the flyer up off of the base.

8. To exit, the spotter continues to support the flyer's waist. The flyer straightens her legs. The base moves her arms into Dagger. The flyer locks out her arms and holds hands with the base inside of the flyer's legs.

9. Together, the spotter and base bend their knees slightly. As they stand up quickly, the base will shrug through her shoulders. She will extend her arms above her head and back slightly to help the flyer come off the base's shoulders and onto the ground.

LET'S GET READY TO TUMBLE

Some cheerleading routines include tumbling. Cartwheels, roundoffs, and handstands are all part of an advanced cheerleader's tumbling routine. A coach or adult can help you or your squad learn these tumbling moves.

HANDSTAND

Handstands are a great way to show off a squad's tumbling skills. They also prepare cheerleaders for more advanced skills. Do not attempt any other weight-bearing skill until you can hold a handstand for at least 3 seconds. Start out by practicing your handstands against a wall. When you feel more comfortable, do these with the help of an adult or spotter.

1. Stand with your legs together and your arms reaching overhead.

2. Step forward with one leg in a deep lunge.

3. Hinge forward to bring your hands down onto the ground. Straighten your arms as you lift your back leg into the air.

4. Spring off your bent leg. Swing both legs high into the air, bringing them together. Point your toes. Be sure to keep your head in the neutral position. This will prevent your back from arching. Make sure you keep your torso in a tight, hollow body position.

5. To exit, bring one leg down at a time. Stand up with both arms up in the air.

Make sure to keep your back safe during handstands.

Pull your belly button in toward your spine when you do handstands.

CARTWHEEL

Once you've mastered the handstand, a coach or adult can help you get to work on the cartwheel.

1. Start with your hands down by your sides. Then bring your arms by your ears and lock them in Touchdown.

2. Lunge to the left. Bring your left hand down toward the ground. Kick your right leg up into the air as you bring your right hand down. Try to open your legs wide into splits when they are in the air.

3. Bring your right leg down to the ground as your left hand lifts away from the ground.

4. Bring your left leg down to the ground. Bring both arms up to the sky to finish in a lunge facing the direction you started in.

ROUNDOFF

Once you've become an expert at the cartwheel, try a

roundoff. Ask a coach or adult to be your spotter while you learn.

1. Start with your arms at your ears locked in Touchdown.

2. Take a deep lunge the same way you do for a cartwheel.

3. Reach your arms to the floor in front of your lunged foot. At the same time, kick your back leg up. Quickly follow with your other leg. Snap your feet together at the top into a handstand.

4. Keep your shoulders down and back, and your arms locked out. You should be in a tight, hollow body position.

5. Snap both feet down to the ground. Land with bent knees facing the direction from which you came. Rebound from the floor by pushing through your toes and bouncing as high and as straight as you can.

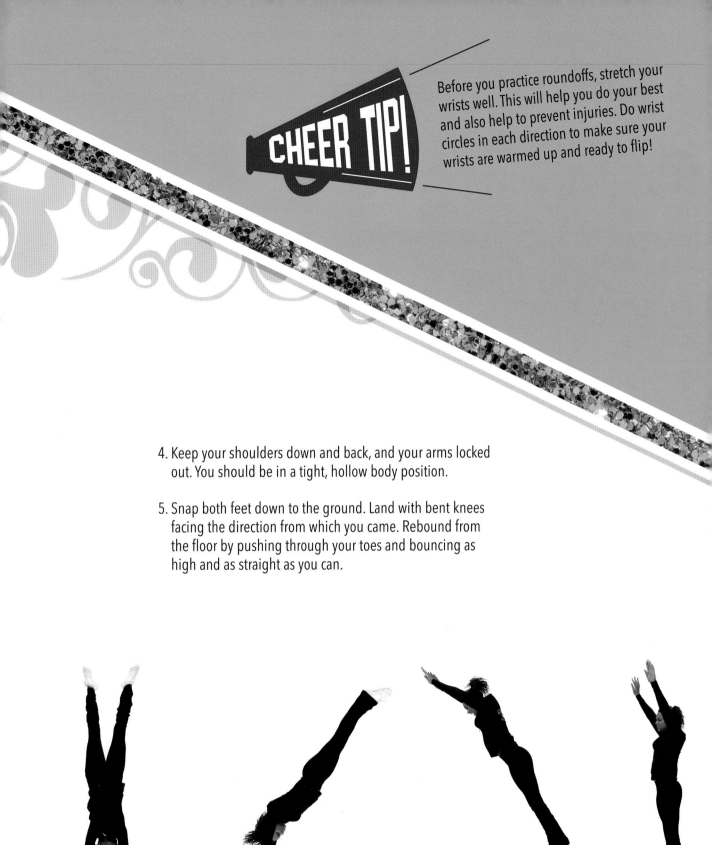

SNACK ATTACK

Fuel your flips! Make sure to eat healthy, nutritious, low-sugar, and low-fat snacks during the day. Try out one of these recipes for a game-day snack. And remember to drink plenty of water.

SMOOTH MOVES SMOOTHIE

An avocado might sound like a strange addition to a sweet smoothie, but it's delicious and creamy. Plus, it packs a punch of protein to keep you energized.

1 avocado, pitted

½ cup low-fat milk

½ cup orange juice

¾ cup frozen raspberries

Mix ingredients together in blender until smooth. Pour into a glass and enjoy.

TOE TOUCH TRAIL MIX

Bring a bag of this trail mix with you on game day in case you need a healthy pick-me-up!

½ cup almonds

½ cup raisins or dried cranberries

¼ cup sunflower seeds

¼ cup chocolate chips

Put all ingredients into a bag and seal. Shake and enjoy.

READ MORE

Hunt, Sara R. *You've Got Spirit: Cheers, Chants, Tips, and Tricks Every Cheerleader Needs to Know.* Minneapolis: Millbrook Press, 2012.

Webber, Rebecca. *Varsity's Ultimate Guide to Cheerleading.* New York: Little, Brown, and Compay, 2014.

Welsh, Piper. *Cheerleading.* Fun Sports for Fitness. Vero Beach, Fl.: Rourke Educational Media, 2013.

INTERNET SITES

FactHound offers a safe, fun way to find Internet sites related to this book. All of the sites on FactHound have been researched by our staff.
Here's all you do:
Visit *www.facthound.com*
Type in this code: 9781491452035

 Check out projects, games and lots more at
www.capstonekids.com

INDEX